Private Hunger

Akron Series in Poetry

Akron Series in Poetry
Elton Glaser, Editor

Barry Seiler, *The Waters of Forgetting*
Raeburn Miller, *The Comma After Love: Selected Poems of Raeburn Miller*
William Greenway, *How the Dead Bury the Dead*
Jon Davis, *Scrimmage of Appetite*
Anita Feng, *Internal Strategies*
Susan Yuzna, *Her Slender Dress*
Raeburn Miller, *The Collected Poems of Raeburn Miller*
Clare Rossini, *Winter Morning with Crow*
Barry Seiler, *Black Leaf*
William Greenway, *Simmer Dim*
Jeanne E. Clark, *Ohio Blue Tips*
Beckian Fritz Goldberg, *Never Be the Horse*
Marlys West, *Notes for a Late-Blooming Martyr*
Dennis Hinrichsen, *Detail from* The Garden of Earthly Delights
Susan Yuzna, *Pale Bird, Spouting Fire*
John Minczeski, *Circle Routes*
Barry Seiler, *Frozen Falls*
Elton Glaser and William Greenway, editors, *I Have My Own Song for It*
Melody Lacina, *Private Hunger*
George Bilgere, *The Good Kiss*

Private Hunger

Poems by
Melody Lacina

The University of Akron Press
Akron, Ohio

 First Edition 2002.
02 03 04 05 06 5 4 3 2 1

All inquiries and permissions requests should be addressed to the publisher, The University of Akron Press, Akron, OH 44325–1703

LIBRARY OF CONGRESS CATALOGING-IN-PUBLICATION DATA

Lacina, Melody, 1958–
Private hunger : poems / by Melody Lacina.
p. cm. — (Akron series in poetry)
ISBN 1-884836-88-7 (pbk. : alk. paper)
I. Title. II. Series.
PS3612.A345P75 2002
811'.6—DC21

2002009181

Manufactured in the United States of America.
The paper used in this publication meets the minimum requirements of American National Standard for Information Sciences—Permanence of Paper for Printed Library Materials, ANSI Z39.48–1984. ∞

Cover design by Jodi Arment.
Cover illustration: Detail from *The Persimmon Tree* by Sakai Hōitsu. Used by permission of The Metropolitan Museum of Art, Rogers Fund, 1957. (57.156.3) Photograph © 1999 The Metropolitan Museum of Art.

To my mother and father

Contents

I

II

I

WHAT I BELIEVE IN

I believe in dark chocolate and salt on the lip
of a margarita glass. I believe in daylight
savings time, dressing babies in bright colors,
and cremation. Writing comes before cleaning.
White paint needs a little cream. Never
stick a fork in a plugged-in toaster.
I don't believe anyone nailed anywhere
will rise. I believe in the underside.
I believe in everlasting soul but not in
talking about it, in being quick
to start and slow to finish. I believe in
the rhythm and off-rhyme of the ordinary.
I would never name a dog Prince. I would never get
a sex-change operation. I would never put nuts
or raisins in carrot cake. Don't live inland
without a river. Don't forget your roots.
What I believe in is simple
architecture, thrust and arch, the bitter-
sweet smell of sex. I don't believe love is
a two-way street but a median strip
with traffic. I believe in being kind.
Remember what you can and make up the rest.

BITTERSWEET

No one here knows what it is.
Not the adjective, common enough,
but the noun, brittle branches
clotted with berries, berries
like small hearts that pulse
out of the fruit's orange skin.
In autumn, bittersweet grows
between the soy and corn fields
my father used to plow. Forty years
the farm's been gone now. Still
he drives the old roads and eyes
the harvest as if the yield,
each acre, matters. Mostly he watches
the birds, bright finches skittering
toward the timber, hawks
lifting from fence posts driven
deep as a grave to last. And because
he remembers how my mother loves
the vine with its blood berries, how she
sings above the sharp snags and makes
them beautiful in a wood bowl,
my father looks for the bittersweet
to untangle from the barbed wire, break
gently, and carry home.

CORN

More common than roses,
corn grew up with us in backyards and vacant lots
like so many neighborhood kids. On Sunday afternoon drives,
Dad could point out cornfields even when the tongues of shoots were
barely aboveground. By the time stalks resembled spines
and leaves waved to us in slow greeting,
he was already gauging acreage yields like the farmer
he used to be. In August, his best friend Bob
loaded our Buick's trunk with bags of corn.
We shucked it on the back porch steps
while Mother set water to boil. Steam rose
from the platter on the supper table.
Night after night, we mouthed corn like harmonicas.
We couldn't get enough of it.
Out on Jensens' farm, we climbed up to the corncrib.
Sun sifted through the weathered boards; the ladder's wood
was rough. At the top of the ladder at the edge
of the crib, we scooped up handfuls of dusty
ocean. We had never seen the ocean.
We had never seen so much corn. It trickled
between our fingers, cooler and smoother than water.
We touched it again. We jumped.
The sudden cloud above the corn reminded us of breath
in winter. It drifted toward the rafters
where swallows rearranged their wings.
In the corn we swam in languid circles. We wore its sediment
like a second skin. Later someone told us
how we could have died there:
our bodies dragged down like reluctant stones,
our throats filled with dry air, then corn.

HOW I GOT MY NAME

My father's family brought the last name
like luggage from Czechoslovakia,
the hard consonants picked over
and dropped at Immigration
where officials slurred the vowels.

The middle one is simple, namesake
of my mother's second sister
who died while still a child.
Pneumonia. My mother knew
when her mother out of the ordinary
stood waiting on the corner
at the end of school.
It should have been me,
Great-grandma Ray whispered,
as if death had come to the right house
but knocked on the wrong bedroom door.

Melody, my first name,
owes nothing to anybody
except my parents. No, they aren't
musicians, though they like music
well enough: my mother humming
old hymns in the kitchen,
my father sorting the trills
of cardinal and finch.
When I ask them why they chose my name,
they say, *The way it sounds.*
Before memory and roots, the unreasonable
singing.

RED CROSS LESSONS AT CITY PARK POOL

My mother never learned to swim, so we did,
my sisters and me, every summer
for two weeks. It was always early morning,
always cloudy. At the gate,
someone dressed in something warm droned
name after name, getting most of them wrong.
They made us take showers
without heat. They made us wait
huddled on the deck, blue-lipped,
until our teachers said
Get in. My oldest sister was
a natural, even took lifesaving and
synchronized swimming. She learned to sink
to music, one leg up like a periscope.
My other sister had a steady stroke.
I was afraid of the deep end
the summer I got Connie. Connie stood
dry on the lip of the pool, mean towel
cinched at her waist. Dark glasses shrouded
her eyes that could have been looking anywhere.
They were looking for mistakes.
I dreamed of the ten-foot marker, the diving boards
like knives. I said I was sick.
My mother said nothing. But next day
she tugged me from bed, determined.
Connie was still by the deep end.
To here, she said. The pool was a mouth
that could swallow me. I pressed

myself down the ladder, pried my fingers
from the rungs. Would my arms forget
everything? Connie watched me swim
past what I couldn't do. *To here.*

HORSE

Not the animal but the game we played
shooting baskets in the driveway.
We took turns shot by shot
until someone sank one,
then the rest of us had to make it
in exactly the same way—
left-handed, behind the back, however
the skillful or lucky one had played it.
Penalty for missing: a letter,
H, and with each strayed shot another
until a horse with all its hooves
stood facing me on the makeshift court.
Some days I could've ridden away
on disappointment, it seemed that sturdy.
Still, I didn't always lose.
Times when my ball didn't need the rim,
when the net was there for the sweet sound
of the drop and the little dance the rope made.
Grace. A different kind of animal
I recognized before I knew its name.

MILK

We could have been a commercial:
strong bones, strong teeth, the carton
bright on the table. Mother carried gallons
from the grocery store to our kitchen
week after week, the clerks exclaiming
we must have company, but really
it was just our family drinking.

Dad was a driver for the dairy.
Before the sun, he'd rise and do things.
Shower, coffee, the uniform shirt
with *Ken* embroidered across his heart.
Then the short blocks' walk to the truck.

Once he took us there to climb up
the way he did every morning. I loved it.
The semi cab red above big tires, milk crates
rattling, I imagined, in back.
He never said how much it hurt him—
the roads that jarred his spine, his hearing
damaged by the constant noise.

No, at supper milk was good.
We drank it with meat and potatoes,
chocolate cake when we were lucky.
How could I know there was harm in this world?
We licked off our wicked white mustaches
and held out our glasses for more.

WITH ONE EYE

My grandpa could work machinery,
drive a car, watch baseball on TV.
He never seemed troubled by his loss,
though by the time I was old enough to know
the story, he'd had years to get used to it.
An accident at the plant. A valve
broke open and sprayed ammonia
in his eye. Instead of running for help,
he stayed, wrenched the valve shut,
then went. No one else hurt,
no other damage, but his eye burned
beyond saving. Mother didn't say
how long he took to recover.
At first I thought he was brave, risking
so much to keep the rest from danger.
Later I reconsidered. Foolish,
such a sacrifice, and maybe for nothing.
Why couldn't some other worker have stepped in?
Later still, I thought again.
An ordinary man, my grandpa,
who fixed the thing he was able to fix
and lived with what couldn't be mended.

GOOD

I didn't have to try very hard
as a child. Being good seemed a family trait.
I memorized multiplication tables,
ate everything on my plate, and went
to bed from TV without whining.
Even at thirteen, troubled
in the usual ways of that age,
I didn't cause much trouble.
Goodness embedded in my bones.
Later, when I wanted a little danger,
each willful change felt like breaking—
no, the good bones not broken but hinged
and pressed to bend for the first time.
Snap with the gin and tonic,
snap snap with the act of sex.
Pain, and the pleasure of my body
loosening, and *good* opening up.

LEMONADE

Two girls sell it on the sidewalk
a quarter a cup. Cheap memory.
I am twenty again, summer,
in my first apartment on Dodge
with walls so thin someone
put a fist through the kitchen closet
years ago in a fit of pique
or drinking. No sign of the damage.
The friend I live with is
learning to cook. Over and over
we eat vegetables before meat,
her timing not yet right.
Everything tastes delicious.
After, we sit on the back steps
away from the leftover heat of supper
and watch Dan and Otis play Frisbee
in the grocery parking lot, nearly empty
this time of evening. They're good.
They catch things I wouldn't bother
reaching for. Ice rattles
as I sip my Strip-and-Go-Naked.
Lemonade and vodka.
I wear an old T-shirt, my nipples
tight against the cotton.
I don't take it off,
though I like to think a man
would like me to. Dan and Otis
come sweating up the steps and eye me

with what I hope is hunger,
but maybe they're merely thirsty,
their game over for the night.
My drink is tart. I hold out what I have.

TWENTY-ONE

To say that I came late to sex
makes it sound as if I missed a call
for supper, the family waiting
hungrily behind the plates of cooling beef.
Really, didn't it feel at times like
everyone I knew had already
eaten? What a meal. Their bodies
happy, mingling.
Not that I was holding out
for love, I wasn't sure,
but I wanted something more than
opportunity, feeble gropings
on the riverbank or behind
a locked door in the dormitory.
When it happened,
I had to believe in luck—
what else could explain it?—the way
a woman betting with eleven will draw
finally the jack she needs.

TORNADO WARNING

August. Day after day wearing heat
like a drenched coat. Then sudden stillness, and sky
the color of an old windshield tinted green.
Sirens tell us what we already know.
My mother cradles the small bodies
of Hummels in towels, carries them
tenderly to the basement. The Bohemian crystal
she wraps as if it were children,
while my sister and I fill our arms with family
photograph albums. Everything else we leave.
Replaceable, my mother says. *Call your father.*
My father stands in the driveway, shaking change
in his pockets and scanning the dark
lip of cloud just above the horizon.
Any minute now a funnel
could lick the landscape clean as a plate.
No sign of worry. He makes this uncertainty
ordinary, like a farmer waiting for rain.
I want the simple faith that keeps him
outside looking up, trusting the weather
to turn and spare us.

CARDINALS

It didn't matter if they lost or won,
my grandfather followed the team.
He could name the players, catcher to field,
and complained when the sportscasters chattered.
Just call the game, he'd say.
If he'd been a spitter, he would have spat.
Instead, he bit his pipe stem hard
and tightened his grip on the bowl.
One bad winter—nothing to do with pitch or hit—
he fell and broke his hip. Who knows
why hope is lost in any season.
Outside, the other cardinals
did their best to coax him to the window.
He turned away. Their bright wings for no reason.

FALL

When Grandfather fell in the bathroom,
Mother wasn't there to catch him.
It was one of those hours before morning,
one of those times he dragged
himself from awkward sleep. Maybe he tried
to brace his body on familiar fixtures. Nothing
held him: not the cupboard
with its drawers of unguents and linens,
not the naked plumbing of the basin
or the toilet's chill porcelain, as his hip broke
without warning. Mother found him
crumpled on the floor. He should have died there.
By then the cancer was in his bones.
Mother couldn't bear to leave him.
Chairs beside his bed took her shape
in the hospital, the nursing home.
He seldom spoke. Pain grew
deeper than the snow outside his window
and as constant. He pressed its bitterness
against his teeth. So when he asked her
to remove his ill-fitting plates,
Mother swallowed her revulsion and
did it. Love was that simple.
She drew out what was hurting, tried to rinse it clean.

LETTER TO MY GRANDMOTHER AFTER HER DEATH

We came back to bury you,
all your kids and almost all
their kids, same as years ago
when we buried Grandpa.
That was the last time
we were together, and this
the last time to call your old house
home. Mother and Ruby packed up
room after room, the hallway
full of boxes. Not much worth saving,
but how does anyone let go?
The piano the hardest. If we could forget
your father gave it to you,
or if we could remember
how to play . . . It looked naked
without the rows of photographs, our faces
young and pressed against the glass.
Of course, the sisters argued,
who knows what about—buried grudges
shaken out like blankets
from the cedar chest. Nobody slept
for days. When we finally
took your body to the grave,
we grandchildren carried the coffin.
So light. What were we bearing,
after all? Your features
you left in Norma's face, and Dad

drops his hands in your old gesture.
We lowered the bones and flesh of you
into the earth and walked away
with what matters.

WORRY

Your mother has cancer, so you ask me
what happened when my own mother had it.
Hard to say. I was nine and knew nothing
about illness except the simple ones
that kept me home from school. About dying
I knew less. I have no memory of wondering
why she was away from us. My father
must have told me, or my older sisters,
who might have been happy at other times
to make me scared. Since they'd seen me fret
over such little things as the needle
on the gas gauge dropping, maybe
they were afraid I would panic. I didn't.
I spent those days in the ordinary
whatever of my childhood. It hurts now
to think how close I came to losing her
without a word of love between us,
and without my voice raised once
to any god to save her. What else can I tell you?
I imagine my mother worried hope like a bone.
She bit hard, and lived.

BLUE HEN

What did my grandmother do with it?
Heavy glass in two pieces, head and wings
I lift from the base, an egg
could fit inside just barely.
It's all I have that was hers.
I set it on the stove and wonder
whether a daughter bought it for her.
Child's hands around her mother's
favorite color, sky at dusk before the stars
begin to show themselves. Did this hen
come through the fire that took the farmhouse?
So little saved, my father said.
And so little the neighbors could spare—
pennies dropped in a jar at the general store.
This must be from later, a year less lean
but still wanting. Maybe it held for her
buttons or pins, the ordinary
little things lost in the world.

DEER

Seeing them used to be a gift
of early morning or twilight.
Where cornfields broke into timber,
they stood unmoving in the dim
safe light, so seldom there we knew
it took luck and strain to find them.

Now there are too many. We count
ten one night in the neighbor's yard
and another one startled back
into brush across the lit road.
They have eaten a litany
of what we hate to lose: roses,
geraniums, the new plum tree
Randy planted along the fence.

Ruined, he says. He would shoot them
if he could. Still, who can blame them?
Ground that once held corn holds houses.
Their feet and mouths no doubt confused
by gardens and the strange clipped grass.
How different the tame must taste.

THE HEDGE ROAD

for my father

Finally a day not cold enough to keep us in.
We drive out of town on a road I should know
the direction of. But north and south
all the same to me, no inner compass
like yours in my bones.
Since I've been gone,
they've put up street signs in the country.
You shake your head. Who needs them
here in beans and corn.
Today the fields are full
of snow. We pull on gloves and tighten
scarves across our faces, our few words
muffled by the wool. On this road
years ago, spring, we nearly got stuck
in mud, the Buick's tires spinning.
Ice this morning underfoot.
We walk with practiced gingerness.
No one out earlier than us
but animals—you show me deer tracks,
rabbit, the brush of a pheasant's wing
just before it flew.
In the branches arching over us, cardinals
and the berries of bittersweet
out of season. We've never seen them
this brilliant this late.
These trees are good for fence posts,
you say. *Hard to break.*

Hard, then, to cut, yet you did it,
and drove the posts deep, and strung the wire.
That was before I was born.
Still, by telling me, you make it
something else I can hold on to:
a wing feather, a stone from the road.

WHAT MY MOTHER TAUGHT ME

Fork to the left of the plate,
knife and spoon to the right.
Sweet corn for supper in summer.
Chocolate is good, but bread
with butter is better. Love
the color red—tomatoes, garnets,
a bedroom wall. Never leave home
without a sweater. Walk.
If you have to drive, go slowly,
in a red car. Hurt no one
on purpose. Say what you think
when someone asks and otherwise
be quiet. Know the names
of what grows around you:
cyclamen, oak, red-tailed hawk.
Keep things. Read. Believe
in the soul and the body,
though the first may not be evident
and the latter will break.
Make small stitches when hemming.
Give freely. Be brave.

II

COMPASS

My father wants me to marry
someone with a sense of direction.
He can't believe I don't know north.
In our house it was simple:
the kitchen door was south.
When Mr. Parker made me chart
stars from our winter driveway,
I could remember where to look
for the Hunter, the Sisters,
because the door stood at my back.
These days I'm not sure, that back door
a compass I couldn't pocket.
My father puzzles over this. To him,
losing your way is like losing
your hand. Unthinkable. I try to
imagine a sense of direction
that palpable. A shirt I could put on.
Cotton, with long sleeves, cuffs to roll
north over south over north.
I would wear it like a loose skin.
Skin that could save me
from muttering *hills east, water west*
as I climb to where I am now.

POSTCARD: AUGUST IN IOWA

I could probably write this in sweat,
but the address would smear and make it too hard
to deliver. I'd forgotten how heavy
heat can be. I keep wishing it were a coat
I could strip off, or a wall I could break
a window through. No wonder I love
storms. Not that we can count on rain
to cool or clear up anything—
afterwards the temperature still climbs.
Some things make the weather worth it: Corn
higher than your head in the field, yellow
teeth on the platter for supper. Smile
when you think of me confusing lightning bugs
with stars, this sky wider than the one you know.
Say hello to strong coffee. I miss it
and you. Nights I take off all my clothes,
wishing you were here.

TEGUCIGALPA

My mother learned to say it,
the city where her youngest in a strange tongue
was buying groceries and reading the paper.
She could tell the next-door neighbor
or the friends whose children I grew up with
what countries bordered the country
I was living in, though before I went,
the two of us had to search a map
to find it. She must have memorized
each consonant and vowel as she wrote them
week after week in her intricate hand
on the thin blue airmail paper.
Maybe after a while she began, as I did,
to call it *Tay-goose*—like a new winged thing
whose shape and flight she'd come to recognize
from a distance. What I think of now
is how she made the unfamiliar comfortable
in her mouth, as if by saying the name
she could cross the geography between us
to be home for me when I opened my door.

MCKENZIE BRIDGE

This river carries my sister's married name
the way she carries laundry,
unthinking, to the basement, the concrete floor
that holds earth's chill even in summer.
She tips out her husband's stiff shirts, the cuffs
rimmed with ink and everyday dirt,
her son's baseball shirt heavy with home base
he tried to slide into, her daughter's indigo sweater
just the right shade because her aunt,
my other sister, chose it and knows.
This river is not like the Iowa River
I grew up with, river the color of silt
and lost corn that thickened in winter
to ice I would never trust but some did,
crossing under bridges, testing foot by foot
or maybe running, I never saw them,
only heard. But this river has a bottom
you can believe in, stones of agate, jasper, quartz.
Stones that have names the river calls
as it trips over them. Stones with moss
like the hair of a child learning to float.
And if the stones are tongues, the banks are lips
the trees climb down to. Pines I don't know the names of.
All these trees with needles. Give them thread.

CAMPING AT CALAVERAS

This time the trouble's not bears
but wasps, the ranger tells us.
Every few years it happens,
swarms throughout the Sierra.
We've come a long way, so we don't turn back
because of something as small as wasps.
Easier for the mouth to say *bees,*
and the name so like their noise
it's tempting to lie, and use it.
But Heather, with the certainty of science,
says that only wasps both sting and bite.
The difference matters
when a few get caught in Sharon's shirt
and, frantic, do their damage.
Her shoulder swells
beyond the meager help of ice.
Sooner or later, we all get stung
except Heather, as if wasp knowledge
makes her immune. Nothing to subdue the pain
but beauty: the wind through the pines
loud sometimes as the Stanislaus, and the stars
crowding out the dark above us.
We wake in the morning to a drone
of wasps. As Redda cuts meat at the table,
they cover his hands like gloves.
A different kind of beauty,
and under it, the danger.

THE MIDWEST

We talk about our reasons for leaving
until we all come down to weather.
We're no good at extremes anymore,
though we like living here on the edge
of the country. Still, we miss things:
Thunderstorms. Lightning bugs. First snow.
And we wonder if this sky will ever hold
as many clouds or stars as that one.
But we don't go back.
By now, we're tethered to the ocean,
the strong light, and we like how our bodies move
through them. Though who can be sure this will last.
Maybe our roots will prove more stubborn
and pull us with a private gravity
to finish where we started, in the middle.

DRIVING HOME

Hawk. Hawk. Different hawk.
All the way up the coast, we count them
sunning on the telephone poles,
their feathers bright after rain.
I am grateful for this break
in the weather, for the light
raking the fields of artichokes
and warming the bodies of familiar birds,
birds my parents would point out
every time we left the city,
my father's eye honed by miles
of highway driving, my mother's keen
since birth. For my whole life
and more, they've been together.
We are talking about love.
You tell me of your father's infidelity,
how your mother bore it. You want to believe
you would never hurt someone
or be hurt yourself like that,
but you worry about what we carry
in our blood and bones.
The bones of birds are hollow.
No wonder they can lift and go.
I swear my parents have been happy.

ON THE TELEPHONE

Talking with friends is cheap—
the weather, the work,
the rickety wheel of love,
then *click*, the conversation's over.
But now that I've fallen in love
with someone who lives in Seattle,
my telephone bill keeps rising.
At this distance, we have to use words
to undress each other. *Slip off*
your shoes. Unbuckle your belt. Open
your shirt for me button by button.
We take turns. Passion makes us
lower our voices, lower our hands
and imagine the other one
watching or touching. Outside,
birds black as the lace of my bra
unhook themselves from the phone wire.
Must be they feel our tongues
burning the line between us, heat
that stirs each body to its wings.

IN THE CATHEDRAL AT MONREALE

We crane our necks to look up at the ark
in a sea of mosaics on the ceiling.
We love the paired animals, the dove
that managed to crest the roof peak
despite its wings of stone.
Everything of stone,
though the water seems fluid and the coats,
if closer, would coax us to touch.
We have known each other since childhood
and have crossed oceans before
to be together. Difficult to think
I have almost lost you
more than once, not to the grievances
that threaten any friendship but to death
trying to take you too soon. *Amazing,* you say,
meaning the mosaics. I answer *yes,*
and wonder how the work was ever done,
hard piece after piece after piece.

PENSIONE TORRE BENNISTRA

Off-season in this town,
it's the only place to stay,
so the woman who runs it takes in
what few travelers find the road.
Not much to drive so far for:
a fist of houses, a bank, a store,
one bar with coffee and homemade ices.
What's worth looking at lies below—
the ocean, beautiful even on a bad day,
and on a good one, the woman says,
you can see all the way to Tunisia.
Today is not that clear, but we still stare,
hoping for another continent.
Unconcerned, two men sit mending nets
that must have once been red.
Imagine color rinsing from the rope
with year after year of pitch and pull
through salty water. Imagine these arms
hauling the nets. Empty. Full.
My life is nothing but sacrifice,
the woman tells us. Empty,
full. The men are old and hold
the nets between their toes, their eyes set
not on the horizon but on the everyday
that always needs mending.

UNDER ETNA

The room is so cold
I sleep in my gloves and hat.
The space heater offers nothing but color,
as if the brilliance of its bars
could keep me warm. Orange,
like the lava that years ago spilled
where I walked today. There are pictures:
the ground no longer solid but steaming
churning rock that buried
almost everything. One wall left standing
bears a line that shows how high the lava went,
like the watermark of a flood.
Hard to think of stone as fluid
and capable of burning.
Somewhere down the hall a couple moans
—the man, then the woman—
their bed scraping across the tile.
I imagine the tangle of limbs
and sheets, the blanket at their feet
a low mountain they thrust away from.
I lie still, remembering how desire
can make the body move from its everyday earth
to those moments when skin is almost liquid
and then fire.

THE ROCK ABOVE CEFALU

They call it La Rocca. We climb it
almost by accident, every turn
in the puzzle of streets an incline
until houses run out like pines at tree line
and we're left with nothing
but a dirt path up. What to do but take it.
Along the trail, flowers we can't name
press their last blossoms to dust.
We keep on through the choke and clutter
of weeds and watch the town diminish
beneath us. Such a small place.
And what of our place?
You're too young for the heart attack
you've lived through, and I'm
nearly too old to bear
the children I've always sworn I wanted.
On the edge of forty, we wonder
if we've done our whole lives wrong.
Here we stand in the ruin
of someone else's battlements,
walls put up for war or against it,
and all that's clear is that
even stone can be broken.
Tell me the words for *hard*, for *happy*.
Let's see if I can say them.

COVE IN ZINGARO

To get to water, you have to cross stones
that hurt your feet but are too beautiful
to complain about. You fill your pockets
with careful choices—this one
for its rusty color, this one because it feels
smoother than skin. Years from now,
you'll still want it, that slick rub
between finger and thumb. You long to touch
the blues the water holds, the best ones
farther than you can reach. Here, where ocean
tucks into rough hills, no one can see you,
or if they can, they are strangers
so what they see doesn't matter.
You take off your clothes.
The Mediterranean clearer than bath water
breaks over your feet, so cold
goose bumps in one steady wave cover you
ankle to wrist, and your nipples
come to surprised attention and salute the sea.
What an allegiance. You will yourself deeper,
your whole body small mouths saying *Oh.*

MOSQUITOS AT SCOPELLO

Through air dense as Sicilian bread, their whines
cut like little knives. I should be safe
with the windows closed, but their mean mouths
reach me anyway. It's not their fault,
I know, it's just their nature—
amazing, really, how much hunger
the delicate bodies can hold.
Still, this late at night I'm past wonder,
and without rest forgiveness comes hard.
I can't kill them fast enough.
I tug on the light, plot their dark paths
against the walls, and one by one
press the back of a book
into their backs. No sound
when they die. The stains of what I've done
are not the first to speckle the paint.
This room is full of small deaths.
In the morning, I wake to welts
at my wrist, clear evidence
my murders were for nothing.
True to my nature, I can't stop
fingering each rise of skin—as with lust,
once stung I always want to scratch.

AT SEGESTA

No one but foreign tourists and a busload
of schoolkids eager for the freedom
and heat of summer. Never mind history:
these boys are bored and want to see something
besides ruins. They love my sleeveless shirt
loose with possibility—the swell of a breast
if I lift my arm just right, one move
that would make all the dust and dry talk worth it.
The nervy ones press close and nudge each other,
whispering. I can't understand the words,
but at times like this who needs language.
Adolescent, I know, both their longing and my wish
to startle them, to strip the fabric
from my nipple and watch their simple need
complicate itself. But I'm not that reckless
or willing to dismantle what little bridge this may be
toward true desire. Let them go slowly.
I keep myself almost covered.

COMING DOWN MOUNT ETNA

Some things here are not foreign to me—
poppies sudden in the fields, wisteria
thick as old men's talk in the square.
All day their conversation. I could fall in love
with the younger mouths, with the hands
that can't stay still while the lips
are moving. When a beautiful stranger says
he's named for a Greek god, it's no surprise.
Ruins of those old believers lie everywhere.
Their temples, still standing
or resurrected after quakes and wars,
make me consider again the word *holy*.
But more than the columns with their chisel
and weight, it's the sun breaking through them
that moves me. Light, and the ordinary
offerings of the earth. Yesterday
the ground crumbled beneath my feet—
ash once fire inside a mountain—
but this far down the slope the olive trees
take hold and bear fruit. I know nothing
of any other world.

3 A.M., LISBON

All I want right now is the light
above my head to read by until sleep,
but so many buttons beside the bed
and my fingers unfamiliar.
By mistake I lower, then raise,
the electric window shade.
Its thunder wakes my lover,
who slips on his eye mask and settles
back under the covers, leaving me
alone with my books and muffled traffic.
Where are they going at this hour
seven floors below me in Portuguese?
Beneath me, cool sheets,
and beside me, the Lone Ranger
horseless and naked. I reach for
the phrase book. How to say *horse*
or *ride*? The simple words I memorize
may be gone by morning, lost
in the drift of sleep and dreams,
if I ever sleep, or dream, in this country.

CONIMBRIGA

The Romans left things all over the place.
Here, remains of an aqueduct, a forum,
the waterways for baths—intricate
enough to imagine how the ancients moved
hot to warm to frigidarium.
Most amazing, the stone mosaics
someone pressed down as floor:
meticulous bodies of horses,
elephants, a muscled merman
emerging from the sea. Waves of kids
in matching school hats stare at us.
We are stranger than Romans or stone.
Maybe they will think of us later
as another foreign invasion, this one brief
but breathing, and so close they could have
touched it with a small brave hand.

AZULEJO

In Portugal, they believe in tile.
Not just for kitchens and baths
but for altarpieces, church façades,
the inside walls of railway stations.
While I wait for a train to Guimarães,
I watch the battle of Aljubarrota
blue and white square after square.
And in one of the common churches
bearing his name, Saint Francis preaches
to a school of fish, each tail and fin
bright in the painted water.
Some of the tile is less elaborate,
but still more beautiful than stucco
or stone. They call it *azulejo.*
I want to live in a house with that skin.
I imagine waking up in it
every morning, accustomed to touching
the patterns, the stories—so complicated
yet so familiar I can trace them later
on my lover's back as I whisper to him
azulejo in the dark.

HEAT

That was the summer I went to Spain
and stayed, my Spanish broken
but enough to order *rioja*—
cheap and deep blood-red in the bottle—
and coffee at the same brass counter
morning after morning. Around me,
the quick tongues of strangers and temperatures
my neighbors pressed shutters against.
At noon, instead of closing
out the light, I walked in it,
the lime-rinsed walls of the Albaicín
miraculous burning snow.
I craved heat.
Day and night I looked for evidence
of its rise—the skin's sheen, the soaked sheets,
the shirts and dresses with their crescent
moons of sweat. In the market,
makeshift canopies shielded
the heads of lettuce and fingers
of vegetables and vendors. I wanted
to eat everything. Later,
when I touched myself,
when I parted the bristle of pubic hair
and unfolded my lips, I remembered opening
the dangerous skin of prickly pears—
how sweet the warm meat in the center,
how sticky my hands with juice.

III

WHAT MY FRIEND SAYS WHEN SHE GIVES ME A PERSIMMON

It tastes like your first kiss,
but you have to let it ripen
until you almost think it's too late,
the beautiful bright body spoiled.
That's when it's best, that's when you open up
the flesh, that's when you want to

lay it on your tongue and savor it,
not really like your first kiss but more like
oral sex, though I wouldn't say that
in public. I couldn't eat one
with a stranger with so much
private hunger going on.

RAIN IN JANUARY

When it started, I was glad
to see the sky cloud up with winter
the way it should. I unearthed
my boots, my overcoat, and went walking,
aiming for the puddles like a child
—a kind of game I could play—
impermeable in the rain. Back home again,
I loved sloughing off my coat
like skin, then stepping out of rubber
with its faint damp scent.

Now I'm tired of trying to stay dry.
I close my eyes and remember
how you opened me as if I were all
doors and windows, your fingers and tongue
unlatching me to let the weather in.

ON SEEING A NUDE SELF-PORTRAIT OF IMOGEN CUNNINGHAM

I like to think of her naked
setting up the tripod, adjusting
the camera angle and lens.
She lies on her stomach in the grass,
her face turned away, her hair
a complicated knot at the neck.
Everything is darker than her skin:
the long grass, the leaves
sharp-edged beside her, then
blurring to indiscriminate brush.
Even the sky and dandelions
gone to seed cannot hold light
the way her body can.
That's why she took off her clothes.
Not because it was August
with its brunt of summer heat,
but because she wanted to print
the brilliance we bear on our bones.

STARGAZING

for Tim

Tonight I tilt my head back
with someone else and try to show him
what you've shown me, over and over
the same lit bodies rising
and falling. By now
it should be easy. But I am slow
to learn patterns, so your meticulous map
gets lost in the surge of stars.
Where are the swan's wings,
the Northern Crown, the crooked rungs
of Andromeda? Without that
nebulous ladder, I can't find
the galaxy we saw together.
The stars do what they can.
They keep throwing light.
For you it is enough, this sky
full of old pictures—a sister
hiding behind her siblings,
an uncle with his rifle shouldered,
returning home after a long hunt.
They could be family snapshots
lifted from the album of a woman
you once loved. There, above the trees,
her faint resemblance.

CALL

My friends' mothers keep dying.
Every time I hear of a death,
I call my own mother back in Iowa,
still alive despite the cancer
that could have taken her years ago,
despite the ailments of growing old.
What am I doing so far away from her?
How could work or the ocean
be reason enough? Each loss
a little closer, the most recent
of a friend I've known since I was twelve.
Her voice broke when she told me.
After, I couldn't reach home.
I had to tell myself over and over
my mother was safe. I couldn't rest
until I heard her voice that night on the line,
thick with the sleep I'd woken her from—
my relief so evident, so great
my mother forgave me.

DAMAGE

In bed you hear
the rare but familiar
storm outside your window.
This one more than rain,
the wind behind it
troubling, and you pull
away from each other
to listen. With a river
of space between you,
it can't be your heartbeats
that break up your sleep.
Besides, you don't recognize
the noise. Nothing you have
come through—the ordinary
bliss and sorrow—has made
your hearts sound like this:
the rip, the grinding,
the wrench of a heavy body
reluctantly moved.
                                        The roof.
Not shingle by shingle
but a steady awful
lifting, like a child
peeling back the scab of
a deep hurt not yet healed.
What can you do?
You lie still. Why rise
to damage in the dark?

Sooner or later, morning
will crawl into your rooms
exposed by storm. Then
the salvage. How you reach for
each other across the damp books,
the flooded floors,
the glasses on the counter
waiting to be rinsed.

SKATING

At just below freezing, my age
higher than the temperature. Too old
to learn—too far to fall,
with bones more brittle than ice.
I delay standing by staring at
the cross-stitch of my laces, their tight weave
between hook and eye. There must be fish
beneath us. I imagine them
listless and bored, waiting
for mercury to climb its slow ladder.
None of us would hear
if an impatient one knocked
on the hardened sky, this temporary ground
where even the most skillful
lose their footing sometimes.

I test a blade of my borrowed skates.
So thin. I don't trust things
to hold me. I had a lover once
who took me on his body
cautiously, afraid the weight of my desire
would be too much for him.
This ice is rough. I stutter across its scars.

GRIEF

When Grandpa died,
I took off my glasses to cry
and then couldn't find them,
groping where I thought I had gone,
sofa to table to kitchen counter
and back, my hands on the everyday
life I had made away from my family.
Empty now. And lost, somehow,
the thing I needed to help me see.
I went on that way it seemed for hours.
The man I loved came by, not knowing.
With no such sadness before
between us, we fumbled with comfort,
give and take. What could we do
but turn to our bodies.
I lay on the sofa and let him
touch me until I shuddered, my grief
unbuttoned like a heavy coat.

WASHING THE SHEETS

My friends are having babies.
I don't know that I like it—
their yes, my no.
Big as boats, their bodies
bump into my old desire,
and I wonder if my own biology
will let me wait
a little longer. Tonight,
my month's blood bright and sudden
leaking on the sheet, I think
not *I want a child* but
what a stain. What's left of sex
a thin dry ghost.
In the same bed, hope and grief.
Cold water and hard soap.

THE READING

At the podium, a woman I know.
Her poems dense with the everyday:
an elevator, sex, the gun a friend
unloads and places in her hand.
While she muses about holding death,
I'm hearing every word and wondering
what she's like in bed. I've never
made love with a woman, but I love
our bodies, curves and meat and the sweet
electricity of the nipple.
Of course, desire is more complicated,
more brain than breast or thigh,
which is why I'm so distracted,
attracted to how she makes me think.
Still, I can't deny the physical.
Her voice with the heat of a well-kept fire.
And her hair not like flame but like rust,
as if she'd stood in the rain for days
watching, weathered by what fell.
She wets her fingers to lift the pages,
and I think of licking. I like this unexpected
longing for a woman. No need
to touch her. After all these years
of reading my mind and body one way, enough
to be shaken.

NAVELS

Getting hers pierced was erotic,
Lisa tells us over strawberries.
We lick the juice from our fingers
while she lifts her shirt to show us
the silver loop. I want to watch her
make it move, muscles of her belly
like waves, the way the woman
at the Moroccan restaurant danced,
the cymbals on her fingers tinny
and sweet. In Leslie's backyard
full of women, we're eating sweets
and talking about eating,
so when Cheryl first mentions navels
they could be oranges.
Then the stories: fingers, tongues.
I don't usually get excited by navels,
but with all this talk and Lisa's shirt
rising like a curtain, I'd like to stick
my thumb in one. Look how easily
we build desire, skin and words.
I open my mouth for another bite.

APPOINTMENT WITH THE HAND SURGEON

The hand is my favorite body part.
At sixteen, while other girls
checked out asses and biceps, I examined
the way fingers flexed across a basketball
or tensed at the neck of a pencil.
I fell in love with my sister's hands
meticulous on guitar strings, my father's
seamed with garden dirt, my mother's wrist-deep
in bread dough. Later, each lover's hands
seemed miraculous: scented lavender
or with a trace of axle grease stubborn
beneath the nails, how they could open
champagne bottles, rain-warped doors,
jars, my secret lips.
Now this man takes my hands and tells me
I must learn to be more careful.
As if he were a palm reader.
He's talking about nerves and damage
and changing habits I never considered
dangerous—how I cock my wrist
or hold my pen. Even the pen can hurt me.
Choose fat instead of thin, he says. *Loosen your grip*
on everything. Not fortune-telling
but therapy. This is what I have to live with:
my hands against me and me against my hands,
day after day these small betrayals.

BOWL

I know you don't mean to break the bowl
when you rap the colander against its rim
so vehemently, you must be hungry,
trying to knock loose the last kernels of corn
stuck to the metal, stubborn,
as if they'd grown there, and it doesn't hold much
sentimental value, not like the green one
Great-aunt Ruth gave to Mother who served
apple salad in it every Thanksgiving,
if you'd hurt that one I would have cried,
though I remember the day I bought
this one, midwinter, its blue washing beige
like water's edge at Limantour Beach,
but it breaks so cleanly,
the ceramic an eggshell accidentally cracked
open, corn spilling like yolk,
and you cry out my name as if you mean it,
the way you used to, so how can I say
anything but *Never mind, it doesn't matter*
while I watch your beautiful hands all over
the bowl.

EATING

If the food is good—fresh salmon, say,
or bittersweet chocolate cake—
to be honest, there aren't many things
I like better. Sex, but only with
someone worth the worry and trouble
of contraception, and even then
the timing must be right. Don't get me started
on love. Besides, the best part of sex is all
the mouths, what we choose to do with them:
whose fingers, whose tongue, where, and how many
tastes we can conjure. Okay, forget dinner.
I'm talking meat of the inner thigh,
sweet nibble and bite, I'm talking gravy,
salt and juice in the shallow spoons
we make of our hands. Food and sex.
What else matters? Words.
One more sign of how I'm preoccupied
with mouths—what goes into them,
what comes out. I love rich vowels
cut open at the table, the tines and knives
of consonants. I can't stop eating,
but still this hunger.

PINE

You want a table of it,
simple, solid, something you would find
in your grandmother's kitchen.
In antique shops,
we run our fingers along the wood
you don't intend to buy—oak
hard and unaffordable,
maple, like autumn you can eat on,
teak, from countries you've gone to
without me. We turn to pine.
No use looking seriously,
you're not ready to decide,
still it's good to know what you have
to choose from. Who chose this wood
to be a verb of longing?
Not of love, but of yearning that darkens
and deepens to grief. An old meaning.
I go away from you and think
table. Made from trees that hold their needles
season after season, no matter
how many years.

ONE MORE POEM ABOUT THE DEAD

My friend Tom is sick and tired
of hearing about the dead.
Almost as bad as angels,
he complains, the way they've come
to drift and settle in so many poems.
He may be right, but what's wrong
with our reluctance to let them go?
I fell in love with a dead girl
the summer I was ten,
her gray photograph blurred
on the gravestone. Eva Fanny Kimmel.
I fingered every letter of her name,
the notch in granite between the years,
wanting to believe her alive
back in color across the grass.
I knew better even then.
Still, who's to say we wouldn't revel in
ghosts unexpectedly playing
Ping-Pong or some other earthly game.
Let it be limbo.
Let them bend what is left of their bodies
to step under the lowering pole.
Let them cheat, and touch the ground.

COOKING

He says he has to hang up to stir the soup.
I want to be more important than soup.
Silly, this being jealous of a meal
simmering in a kitchen I can't see,
but who would claim love is reasonable,
especially in its early days, when hunger means
new skin to touch, new tongue and thrust.
Let the broth boil. Let the vegetables
stick and burn. Give me words
hot as the flame he holds the saucepan over.

No. I know better than to believe
desire can be food enough to keep us.
We stop talking and he goes back
to the kitchen, to the lip of the spoon
he'll run his finger along for a taste.
Such a good cook. Later, when I'm with him,
he'll lower the ladle into the pot—
steam rising, mouths open. Then the wait
will be worth it: all our greed on the table
and every bowl filled.

THIRTY-NINE

I make my boyfriend stay away
from my birthday dinner
because I'm not sure I love him
enough to marry him and bear
babies or accidents of intimacy.
He's forty-two and tired
of being patient, his understanding
miraculous, elastic
but stretched as far as it can go.
I don't blame him.
I know what feels missing between us
may be something I carry
unwittingly, like an extra bone—
a wishbone
too deep in my body to break.
On the cake, a single candle.
I think of him touching
the ring on his middle finger,
a simple band of silver
he got years ago from a girlfriend
or in Morocco, he can't recall.
How comfortably he wears
the history he makes of it.
All my years of loving, I have wanted
what I didn't have.
I cup the flame to hold the heat
a little longer before I blow
the candle out, the whole table singing,
hungry for something sweet.

THE ROAD FROM MUIR WOODS

Convinced after so many years that I'm lost
to this place, my parents come out for a visit.
I've never been closer to being settled,
though we don't say that, and I don't say
what's still unsettled.
We head for the redwoods. Dad can't get over
the traffic, nearly bumper to bumper
midmorning. Mom sits in back and points out birds,
trees in blossom, anything good out the window.
Her naming of my everyday a comfort.
On Highway 1, the cars diminish and slow.
Winter, hard storm after storm, has left
the hillsides green. *Beautiful,* Mom says
and says again, while Dad shakes his head
in wonder. In the woods, sun and rain
and the rough bark we reach out to touch.
How much we have all been through.
We take turns standing in front of trees
for pictures. By the time we leave,
the sun is out to stay and we're hungry.
I drive toward food and dark beer I remember,
but true to my sorry sense of direction
I go the wrong way and don't notice
for miles. My parents, used to my not knowing
north from south, laugh and seem not to mind.
Better than eating, this mistake of a road—
bright heather on one hand and water on the other—
as if every turn that I make will be happy.

TALKING TO GOD

My sister's boyfriend swears
you keep tabs on all of us. He means
whether we're good or bad, but I imagine
a bar bill run up for regulars, who knows
when or how much we'll have to pay.
I see you behind a brass counter
wiping up beer and fingerprints, rinsing
glasses over and over. Always the same
bad jokes. Mostly you pretend
to listen, your head cocked as if straining
toward every hoarse request. You pour
whatever you want and the desperate ones,
thirsty for anything, drink it.

But maybe my sister is right,
that you don't count wrongs and kindnesses
on a scorecard, adding or subtracting
in blessed arithmetic. She trusts
you were human once, though she's less certain
about the details: the cross, the cave,
the unreasonable rising. Still, her faith is
a well she can draw from. Where did she get
the pulley and the rope?

Me, I don't know what to think.
I try to believe in spirit
held in everything from blades of grass
to Saturn's rings, but such ordinary
holiness is really more than I am

willing to bear. Give me time.
Faith may be something else I can grow
into, like my sister's hand-me-downs.
Even when we were children, I had to wait
years until what I wanted would fit.

AFTER I DIE

Sell everything. Promise me
an auction, an old guy hollering
prices in a broken yodel,
his voice so rough you'd swear
he used to shuck corn
with his throat. Better yet,
a yard sale. Strangers can finger
bowls and coats and wonder
why I ever bought them and whether
they would like them any better
marked a couple dollars down.
Don't let the quilt go cheap—
Amish ladies in Iowa went blind
stitching it. The bedframe still folds
reluctantly into a sofa,
and anyone who wants a hard
mattress will not mind
how stiff the futon has grown.
Be sure the labels
on the sweaters from Venice
are showing. You know how
people will buy anything
Italian. Give away the books.

Burn the body. Keep the ashes
in a mayonnaise jar,
the way we used to hoard
lightning bugs until they stopped
glowing. When no one is watching,

tap out a handful of the ashes
on the beach at Limantour.
A slow crooked line
behind the tide, as if I were dragging
my toes, complaining how cold
the water leaves the sand.
Then buy plane tickets
with the yard sale money.
Pack the mayonnaise jar
carefully. Unwrap it in what was
my parents' backyard to scatter
bone shards beneath the lilac bushes.
After that go to Spain, and don't forget
the jar. Open it on the first
stone street above the cathedral
in Granada, where an old woman
fierce with her broom will not
look up. Drop what you have
left of me in front of her.
Ashes to dust. And always
someone sweeping.

LOOKING FOR COMET HYAKUTAKE

Nine million miles is nothing
to a star, to any bright body
tethered or loose in the night sky.
The man who first spotted this comet
is as common as the rest of us,
not a scientist but simply someone in love
with the dark and the complicated
patterns we can find in it.
The comet a brilliant flaw
in the pattern. We step outside
the Teacup Lounge with the blues
still humming in our heads and the gin
biting our tongues but no longer bitter.
Where to start? The overturned
bowl of the Dipper, then down
its crooked handle to the unfamiliar
prick and blur of light, as if a child
had drawn a star and deliberately
smudged it. Beautiful thumbprint.
We shield our eyes from street lights
to stare at the luminous
spit of cosmic ice. Whatever the distance,
for beauty, for love, we will cross it.

Acknowledgments

I gratefully acknowledge the editors of the journals and anthologies in which these poems first appeared.

Alaska Quarterly Review: "On Seeing a Nude Self-Portrait of Imogen Cunningham"; *Bellingham Review*: "Skating"; *5 AM*: "Cardinals"; *I Feel a Little Jumpy Around You*: "Red Cross Lessons at City Park Pool"; *Rain City Review*: "Bowl"; *Rattle*: "After I Die"; *River Oak Review*: "One More Poem about the Dead," "Pensione Torre Bennistra," and "Under Etna"; *Spoon River Poetry Review*: "Blue Hen" and "Tegucigalpa"; *Sulphur River Literary Review*: "What My Mother Taught Me"; *Times Ten: An Anthology of Northern California Poets*: "After I Die," "Coming Down Mount Etna," "Compass," "Cooking," "Corn," "Damage," "Deer," "Heat," "Looking for Comet Hyakutake," "Navels," "On Seeing a Nude Self-Portrait of Imogen Cunningham," "On the Telephone," "Pine," "Talking to God," "The Rock above Cefalu," "What I Believe In," and "What My Friend Says When She Gives Me a Persimmon"; *Wisconsin Review*: "Appointment with the Hand Surgeon."

Thanks also to my family and friends, who put up with my telling their stories. I thank, in particular, Tim Edberg for his good ear and great heart; Sharon Fain and my other writing buddies—Times Ten to Tom's group to Stray Poets—for helping me shape these poems, especially Lynne Knight and Laura Horn, who offered comments on the manuscript's first draft; Ellery Akers, Naomi Shihab Nye, and Dorianne Laux, whose teaching and poetry continue to influence me; Mary Vradelis, who threw a book party for me before the manuscript even existed; Elton Glaser for believing in my work and bringing it to press; and Matthew Silverberg, who bravely undertook the task of training me on the computer, keyed my poems when I couldn't, and feeds me in all ways. Finally, my deepest thanks go to my mother, who has praised my voice for as long as I can remember and listens to me no matter what.

About the Author

Melody Lacina grew up in Iowa and now lives in San Francisco. Her poems have appeared in a number of anthologies and journals, including the *Alaska Quarterly Review*, the *North American Review*, and *Rattle*. *Private Hunger* is her first book.

About the Book

Private Hunger was designed and typeset by Amy Petersen. The typeface, Centaur, was designed by Bruce Rogers in 1914. *Private Hunger* was printed on 60-pound Writers Natural and bound by McNaughton & Gunn of Saline, Michigan.